Life's Least Important Questions

JIM PAILLOT

STERLING PUBLISHING CO., INC.
New York

Illustrated by Jim Paillot, of course
Edited by Jeanette Green
Designed by Rhea Braunstein

Library of Congress Cataloging-in-Publication Data

Paillot, Jim.
Life's least important questions / Jim Paillot.
p. cm.
Includes index.
Summary: Presents an assortment of silly questions, funny poems, humorous advice columns, and zany cartoons.
ISBN 0-8069-8074-5
1. Wit and humor, Juvenile. [1. Wit and humor.] I. Title.

PN6166.P35 2002
818.'602—dc21 2001057662

1 3 5 7 9 10 8 6 4 2

Published by Sterling Publishing Co., Inc.
387 Park Avenue South, New York, New York 10016

Distributed in Canada by Sterling Publishing Co., Inc.
c/o Canadian Manda Group, One Atlantic Avenue, Suite 105
Toronto, Ontario, Canada M6K 3E7
Distributed in Great Britain and Europe by Chris Lloyd at Orca Book Services, Stanley House, Fleets Lane, Poole, BH15 3AJ England
Distributed in Australia by Capricorn Link (Australia) Pty. Ltd.
P.O. Box 704, Windsor, NSW 2756 Australia
Printed in China

Sterling ISBN 0-8069-8074-5

Contents

About the Author

Jim Paillot has created scads of illustrations for fun folks like Walt Disney Imagineering, Coca-Cola, *Sports Illustrated for Kids,* Nickelodeon, and Klutz Publishing. He also helped design Port Discovery, The Children's Museum in Baltimore.

Jim gets a lot of inspiration for his silly artwork from his wife, Lisa, and their children, Camden and Roseanna, and their two illogical dogs. They get a kick out of robots, cowboy music, cartoons, pirates, and flowers. They all share a small and noisy house in Kansas City, Missouri. It's easy to find. It's the one with lots of toys in the front yard.

To see more of Jim's artwork, you can go to www.jimpaillot.com or e-mail Jim at jim@jimpaillot.com

To Lisa, My Hero

Introduction

While working on paintings and drawings most of the day there comes a point, for no reason at all, when my mind wanders and I begin to wonder about the important questions in our lives. Questions like: "If the chimp expert, Jane Goodall, observed and studied head lice instead of monkeys—would she still be excited about her job each day?" Or scenarios like this: "It's Thursday night and the Pope is coming over for dinner. He arrives promptly (as usual), but because of a rare DNA defect he is now half Pope and half hammerhead shark. He is cranky and hungry. Do you go ahead and serve the meatloaf or do you send out for a nice tuna casserole?"

I like to suppose that these mind bogglers are among life's most important questions (though you see my publisher thought otherwise).

These silly, mind-boggling questions and situations are meant to tease, tantalize, poke, and annoy that tiny, shrivelled part of your brain that usually lies dormant. It's the odd little chunk of your brain that will never split infinitives, conjugate a verb, or multiply a fraction. But if you're wondering if Barney Fife could beat Urkel in thumb-wrestling (I think he could.) then you've stumbled upon a one of them.

A good mind-boggling question shows up unexpectedly and rarely has a final answer. They are all debatable and hardly any are worth debating. They are from the Misfit Island of questions. And because of that, they are always my favorite kinds of questions. I hope they're yours, too.

Chapter One

Basking in the Glory That Is You

You are a big-shot artist who will be paid insane amounts of money to sculpt five life-size statues of beekeepers. You must choose one medium out of these different possibilities to establish your artistic legacy:

a) Bubble wrap
b) Potted meat
c) Pointy cacti
d) Sacks of hair

One of the most popular ways to spend your time is by being involved with a hobby. Whether building model airplanes or collecting stamps, hobbies can be a good way to unwind. Choose a hobby that's right for you:

a) Making puppets from wet seaweed
b) Constructing nativity scenes inside ham cans
c) Building life-size replicas of the Great Pyramids using snack cakes
d) Collecting chicken teeth
e) Making hammocks from greasy, discarded bicycle chains

Get Noticed! Here's some sure-fire ways to get attention and increase your popularity:

a) Raise a family of sea monkeys in your thermos.
b) Lengthen your fingers by at least two extra joints.
c) Eat a complete package of Oreos and gnaw on a few Slim Jims before going to the dentist.
d) End every statement with, "So says the great and powerful Oz!" Be very dramatic.
e) Superglue yellow Post-It notes to your arms and legs. Occasionally jot down a humorous thought on one of the notes.
f) Insist on being called Chief Wahoo and tether a live American bald eagle onto your shoulder.

You are a strict vegetarian. BUT, you get to eat only once a day, and you get to choose from these scrumptious breakfast meals:

a) Meat Loops
b) Frosted Fish Flakes
c) Count Meatula
d) Lucky Beef Charms
e) Captain Crunch with Pork Berries

You're headed to an authentic western ranch where you'll work from dawn to dusk. Here's your list of chores that must finish before the dinner bell rings. Since you're a greenhorn, you get skip one of these tasks. Choose one:

a) Drive a herd of quail to Dodge City.
b) Clean spittin' tobacco stains from the steers' horns.
c) Tell the head trailhand, Ol' Yellerteeth, that in the last half century, dentistry has made some wonderful advances.
d) Braid the back hair on the biggest, meanest, ugliest mule this side of the Rio Grande.
e) Organize the chickens into a union; then go on strike.
f) Sing "Home on the Range" to a scorpion.

Get Culture. Write a Poem!

Hey, you don't have to be a Robert Frostbite or Henry Wadsworth Longmellon to be a poet.

Just tap into that inner *you*. The poet in you that's just waiting to bust a rhyme. Remember: you don't have to be a mournful recluse to have a meaningful thought. Actually, poems don't even have to rhyme. Then again, french fries don't have to have salt, but aren't they better that way?

Impress your friends or bore the family pet. Fill in the blanks and make like Walt Witless.

A hairpiece is a wad of hair
that would look better on a _*(rhymes with hair)*_.
And if I glued it on my _*(rhymes with nest)*_.
an otter might use it for a nest!

A biker gang rode up and said:
"What's that smell coming from your _(rhymes with said)_?"
Their toothless smiles gave me hope,
and so I told them that it was soap.

An angry pack of wild gnus
decided they would like to wear your _(rhymes with gnus)_.
"I'm size _____," you said.
"And you're size thirty!
Besides, I don't want to get them dirty."

Dear Brainiac,

OK, here's the problem—I like this guy, OK? But I don't know if he likes me back, OK? Like, yesterday my hand "accidentally" touched his while we were passing out graded science tests. I got a "B." Anyway, I almost screamed!!! I don't even know if he noticed that we touched. But he did look at me sort of weird like.

What do I do now?? I am like totally spazzing over this, OK?

Totally in Tuscaloosa

Dear Totally,

It's obvious that this guy is crazy about you. But he's shy. You'll have to make the first move to help bring him out of his shell.

Here's what I suggest: Wait until you both are in a very crowded public place. And then all of a sudden start screaming and flailing your arms as though a thousand spiders were on you. Faint directly in front of him. Now is his chance to be a hero and revive you. Just keep laying there until he makes his move. This works almost half of the time. Good luck!

Dear Brainiac,

I have finally found Mr. Right. He is almost perfect. We laugh and hold hands. We have fun all the time. He is soooo romantic. But there is one problem: my friends don't like him just because he's a savage head hunter. This is no big deal to me. I think everyone should have a hobby. But my friends are all in a huff.

I have agreed to follow your advice. Do I keep him or dump him. Please answer soon because I am starting to notice that he measures my head a lot.

Head Over Heels in Biloxi

Dear Head,

I agree with you. True love is rare and it seems as though you have found a gem. Don't let those envious friends ruin a perfect match. You sound like you have a good head on your shoulders.

Time to let that musical side of you shine. You and your friends are starting a band. You've got the talent. The instruments. And enough room in the garage. All you need is a catchy name for your band, and you're that much closer to your first platinum record. Pick a winner:

a) The Smudgesickles
b) The Backwash Boys
c) Scrambled Eggnog
d) N-Stynk
e) Corndog Blackmail
f) The Gout
g) Festering Licorice
h) The Insensitive Narwhales

You can tell a lot about people by the kind of pet they own and how well they treat it. Especially if the animal is in poor health. Choose one of these lovable but unfortunate pets to cherish:

a) Kiwi bird with a lisp
b) Ant with a stye
c) Barracuda with allergies
d) Limping centipede
e) Condor with a pesky hangnail
f) Python with chronic bad breath
g) Amoeba with a split personality
h) Tapir with a belly rash

Keep a Dream Journal

Some people feel that dreams can offer a glimpse into our unconscious thoughts and tell us a lot about ourselves.

Keep a notebook and pencil at your bedside, and when you wake up, jot down everything you remember about your dreams that night. After a few weeks, you may notice recurring images or people. For instance, do you fly a lot in your dreams? Or are you frequently a cardboard salesman in Topeka?

Everyone's dreams are different. But here are a few common dream themes and their interpretations or loose translations:

Dream: You strike out during a school softball game, and your team trades you to a school in Rochester for a bag of softballs.

Translation: Travel is a common dream theme. It can help build confidence and character. Go with it!

Dream: You are an incredibly popular rock star. Except all your fans and groupies are codfish.

Translation: You are up to your gills in schoolwork. Don't let your studies flounder.

Dream: Your new hairstyle is so large and out of control that it becomes a major attraction at Disneyland.

Translation: Great! You're different and now you'll be popular . . . at least in your dreams.

Dream: You are out in public wearing only your underwear.

Translation: This could mean that you are a big show-off. For goodness's sake, get dressed before you go to bed!

Dream: You enjoy the same kind of music as your parents and grandparents.

Translation: Whatever you do—don't sleep!!!

Down on your luck? Life not treating you well? One of the best ways to make yourself feel better is to help others who are even less fortunate than yourself. Donate your precious time to one of the worthy charities below:

a) People for the Ethical Treatment of Grape Stompers
b) SPMA—Society to Prevent Mothball Abuse
c) National Association of Beady-Eyed Neighbors
d) Hope for Lactose-Intolerant Canadian Mounties
e) The League of Nine-Fingered Knife Sharpeners
f) The Monks with Lobster Claws Instead of Hands Foundation

Sometimes we get caught on this great big hamster wheel we call life and forget to sloooooooow down. Take . . . a . . . breath . . . Relax. Meditate. Choose one of these paths to inner peace:

a) Lay in a gentle, soothing tub filled with mashed bananas and find your inner monkey.
b) Perform the beautiful and graceful dance of the egret. And then catch a live perch in your teeth.
c) Aromatherapy—Lay upon a cushiony bed made from old tennis shoes and dirty, mildewy socks.
d) Yoga—Relax by bending and twisting your arms and legs into unbelievably odd positions. Later, have a friend untie you.

Learn to Be a Palm Reader

Palmistry is an ancient art that has been practiced for more than 5,000 years. Every hand is a map of life and can reveal much about you or your friends. With this beginner's course in palm reading, your pals will be amazed as you gaze upon their clammy paws and tell them their life story.

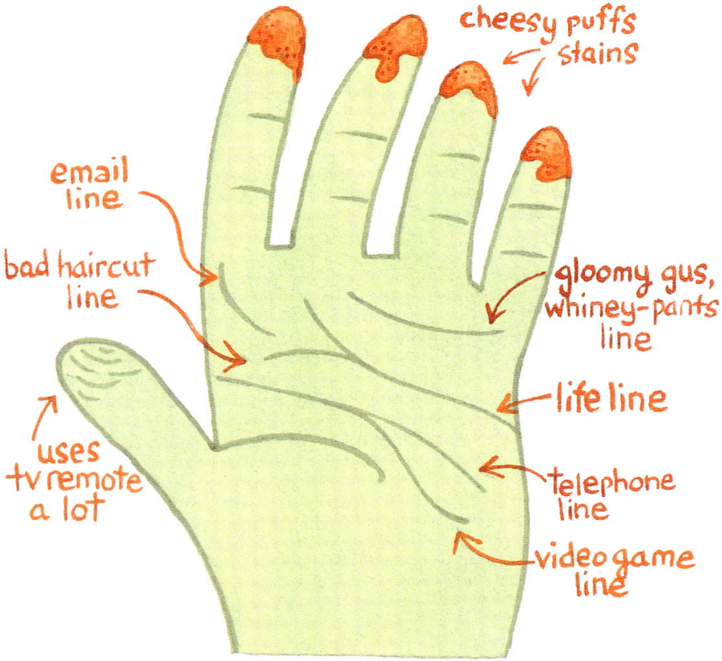

For Advanced Palm Readers Only!

Once you've mastered basic palm reading, you'll make lots of friends by tossing their shoes and socks aside and begin analyzing their feet. Like hands, the soles of our feet are a good indication of where we've been and where we're going in life.

Remember, not everyone is as deep and spiritually aware as you are. So try not to tickle.

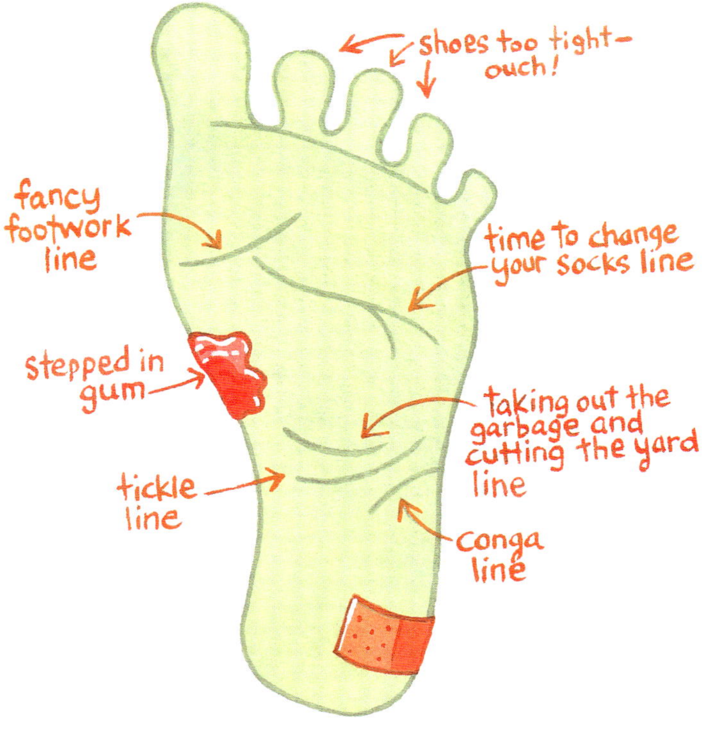

Guess Who's Coming to Dinner

Is there anything more exciting than hosting your own dinner party? This is a chance to show that you're the Host with the Most! Crank up the Time Machine because you have a chance to invite these famous folks from history and fiction to your house for dinner.

Choose two groups of guests to dine together . . . with you. And choose two groups of dinners to serve. Remember, a good party is defined by a lively guest list and scrumptious food.

The Guests

a) Colin Powell
Atilla the Hun
Barney Rubble
Joan of Arc

b) Tonto
Snidely Whiplash
Mozart
Annie Oakley

c) Helen Keller
Lassie
Blackbeard the Pirate
Einstein

d) Princess Di
Dr. Frankenstein
Barney Fife
Sherlock Holmes

The Food

a) *Main Course:* Pepper Noodles Floating in Light, Creamy Tartar Sauce
Side Dish: A Small Bowl of Mayonaisse Lightly Sprinkled with Bacon Bits
Dessert: Garlic Ice Cream

b) *Main Course:* Beef-Jerky Pot Pie
Side Dish: Deep-Fried Corn on the Cob
Dessert: Cheese Ball

c) *Main Course:* Breaded Jellyfish Topped with a Medallion of Flounder
Side Dish: Sardine Pudding
Dessert: Plankton Jelly on Crackers

d) *Main Course:* Chicken-Fried Beets with Shredded Coconut
Side Dish: Popcorn Balls Dipped in Beef Gravy
Dessert: Sugared Gecko

Tiger Spirit
Today:
·Tongue
·jello
FORM 1 LINE

Chapter Two

Zen and the Art of Spitball Maintenance

Thomas Edison invented the lightbulb, phonograph, and movie projector, and he had over 1,000 other patented inventions. While Thomas was a pretty smart guy—what did his not-so-genius brother, Loogy Edison invent?

a) The electric washrag
b) The lunchmeat necklace
c) The steam-powered bookmark
d) The sandpaper harmonica
e) The self-propelled While-U-Sleep nose-hair clippers

You are giving an oral report called "The Magical Story of Styrofoam." This riveting saga is not complete without which of the following facts. Choose one:

a) Elephants are often hunted illegally for their Styrofoam tusks.
b) Early submarines were made entirely of Styrofoam and sea sponges.
c) The collapse of the Incan empire can be traced back to the use of Styrofoam weapons.
d) John Steinbeck's classic novel *Of Mice and Men* was originally titled *Of Mice and Styrofoam*.

Move over, Arbor Day! Celebrate another culture's rich history! Choose a holiday below and have a party!

a) Celebrate Shin-Jolly, as they do in the island nation of Vanuatu, by whacking each other's shins with dry spaghetti.
b) The festival of Grist in Zimbabwe is celebrated by citizens greeting each other by a dry, hoarse, throat-clearing, hacking bark.
c) New Guinea's unofficial Head-on-a-Stick Day can often last for fifteen hilarious and then eventually tedious days.
d) A local holiday in Estonia begins by placing a frozen halibut down your shirt and then cinching up your belt until you cannot feel your legs.

The Chess Club sponsors Wrestle-Mania Virtual-Reality Day! Choose your tag-team partner:

a) Ghandi
b) Mother Theresa
c) Barney Fife
d) Horschak from the TV show "Welcome Back, Kotter"

Required Reading! You need to give a book report and short musical skit based on one of the following literary classics:

a) *Paint Your Aardvark*
b) *The Expanded History of Barbed Wire*
c) Abraham Lincoln's *Nuttiest Limericks*
d) *The Winston Churchill Fruit-Bat Recipe Book*
e) Oscar Wilde's *Big Book of Sailor Knots*

The first President of the United States to wear contact lenses was Lyndon B. Johnson. Which of these other "firsts" are true?

a) Shakespeare's first play to be performed onstage was called *Much Ado About Gilligan.*
b) The first oven mitt was made of cat hair—with the rest of the cat still attached!
c) On the first version of Indian-head nickels, Geronimo was shown parasailing onto the back of a grazing buffalo.
d) In an early version of Edgar Rice Burroughs' classic, *Tarzan of the Apes,* Tarzan was raised in an ant farm.

You're the Hall Monitor this week. The olfactory smell-o-meter has been indicating a strange life force—and odor—in locker #105. You're on duty, so you must investigate. As you open the locker an incredibly disgusting spawn from the sewer wraps you in it's tentacles and has taken a liking to you. Now what's your plan:

a) Give him a breath mint.
b) Nominate him for your school mascot.
c) Smuggle him onto the bus and take him home.
d) Smile and say, "Oh, is this your locker? I love what you've done with the color scheme!"

Old Hickory was the colorful nickname for Andrew Jackson and Abe Lincoln was called the Rail Splitter. Match these other well-known Americans to their descriptive but not-often-used nicknames:

1) John Wayne
2) Shirley Temple
3) Mark Twain
4) George Washington
5) Jesse James
6) Davey Crockett
7) Betty Ford
8) Elvis Presley

a) The Slithery Bumpkin
b) Ol' What's His Name
c) Mr. Waxy Build-up
d) The Limping Pelican
e) Jittery Shrew
f) Lunchbox Belly
g) Old Iron Noggin'
h) Rusty Lugnut

Come 'n' Get It!

Mmmmmm! For most students, lunchtime is a time to visit with friends and have a good meal. But not at your school. Head Chef Argylia Creamcorn has outdone herself and is giving you a wide variety of yummy choices to choose from.

Choose at least one yummy dish from each of the major food groups. We'll let you imagine your own (in)edibles.

Leathery Food Group
The Cow Knuckle Bucket Supreme
Soy Burger Pattie on a Rope
The Mystery Meat Bundle
The Big Block O'Fish Parts

Slimy Food Group
Clam on a Stick
The Hungry Kid Snail Basket
Seaweed Snack Pack
Liver and Eggplant Burrito Wrap

Oozing Food Group
Canned Monkey Dumplings
The Lazy Butcher Pot Pie
Cottage Cheese and Oyster Pudding
Sea Cucumber Surprise

Liquidy Food Group
Day-Old Pickle Juice
Ham-Flavored Skim Milk
A carton of "Bacon Grease Chug-a-Lug"
Buttermilk and Shrimp Blend

You're vice president of your school's Explorer Club. While retracing the historic route of Lewis and Clark, your class loses the trail and are captured by the legendary lost tribe of Bigfoot Indians. Chief Rotting Hangnail will let you and your classmates go free if you first do one of the following:

a) Perform the Sacred Dance of Freedom by repeatedly cracking your funnybone against a rock.
b) Walk the Trail of Tears. Everyone must slowly walk by each oversized warrior as he exhales a lifetime of fish and onion gruel directly into your face.
c) Sing the "Gurgling Song of Friendship." As you wail this incoherent song-noise, the Bigfoot braves spoon feed you large amounts of watery cornhash.
d) Perform the Oath of Brotherhood. Your class and all Bigfoot warriors mumble this important oath together. Then you catch and shave a wild badger.

It's never too early to prepare for college. You must take one of these exciting courses to decide if college is right for you.

a) Whatever 101

b) Studies in Soap and Washrags: An Idea Whose Time Has Come

c) Twinkies and Pizza: Nutritional Breakthroughs

d) Frisbee through the Ages

e) "I Know Everything and I'm Willing to Share," Basic College Relationship Studies

f) Spitball Physics

g) Piercing Ins and Outs

h) The Feng Shui of Skateboard & Surfboard Placement

i) Loose Clothing, Tight Budgets: Economics for Real People

j) "They Just Don't Understand Us!" (weekly lecture series)

k) Probability & the Billiard Ball

Oh No!!

A seemingly harmless experiment in biology class has gone horribly wrong. BUT, you have miraculously obtained superhuman powers, and you can now take up the fight against evil in your school. Choose the superhero you are to become:

a) Captain Custodian! Your left armpit is lightning and your right armpit is thunder. Fighting crime can be smelly work.

b) Armed with only an A.M. radio and a neck that can turn 360 degrees—nothing eludes the wary eyes of the Bus-Driving Ninja!

c) Mr. Ooze! Crawling forth from the cafeteria—you were yesterday's meat surprise. Now you're today's pungent crimefighter!

d) When the tardy bell rings, the bad guys scurry from the halls like cowardly roaches. But nobody escapes the justice of The Mysterious Hall Monitor!

You're on a class field trip to the local TV station. Chet Roberts, the celebrated news anchor and farm reporter, hears you gossip with a friend while touring the station. He thinks you have real talent and wants you to audition as weekend anchor for "Kids' News and Views"! Choose one of these breaking news stories to report on:

a) A local outbreak of Radioactive Mad Cow—Bad-Hair-Day Disease. (All livestock should seek shelter in the basement.)
b) Aliens take over the Speech Club at school. Club members' reaction: "No Comment."
c) Mysterious and putrid Swamp Gas seeps into school gym class. The situation smells rotten.
d) Students protest the closing of the Photography Club. Pictures at eleven.

Every school needs a school song. At least that's what your school principal thinks. You have been chosen to put your colossal musical talent to work and create an inspirational masterpiece. By the way, your masterpiece is due tomorrow morning. Choose any of these opening lines to get started:

a) "Oh, *(your school here)*!
You have dingy halls
And creaky lockers
And teachers who belong in rockers!"

b) "Broken teeth and hallowed eyes
From leathery pizza and meat-brick surprise.
We students at *(your school here)* are an
incredible bunch
Because we've survived another
lunch!"

c) "Our school looks like
Stonehenge.
This place is a mess.
But this school is the best,
As long as you don't
count the rest."

Og is not only your gym teacher—he's a Neanderthal man from the past. But at least he's a fair and thoughtful caveman. He's letting your gym class decide today's activity. Choose one:

a) Stare at a campfire and grunt.
b) Pick small insects from each other's hair.
c) Scratch yourself.
d) Scratch everyone else.
e) Stare at the sun.
f) Gnaw on a rock.

Homework Boggler

Complete the following well-known phrase of American history: "In 1492, Columbus sailed the ocean blue . . ."

a) ". . . and dined for days on fish-head stew."
b) ". . . with a raggedy map his first mate drew."
c) ". . . and then turned around without a clue."
d) ". . . and then seasick Chris began to spew."

Birth of a Nation

Complete the following inspirational battle cry that the Colonists used in the Battle of Bunker Hill during the Revolutionary War. "Don't fire until you see the whites of their . . ."

a) bellies
b) penguins
c) crumpets
d) epiglottis
e) venom-dripping fangs
f) cell phones

Everyone knows that pirates are heartless, bloodthirsty thieves. Or are they? Before the notorious Blackbeard made himself a legend, he was known as Horace the-Timid-Wren Dren. He served as first mate and ship's librarian on which of the following not-so-scary pirate ships:

a) The Sea Gerbil
b) The Golden Welt
c) The Rickety Flounder
d) The Dry Heave
e) Quiche Lorraine

Your school is part of the foreign-exchange student program. Because of your good grades and popularity, you have been chosen to tutor one of these exchange students for the entire semester. Pick one:

a) **Shadrock Bubonic** A quiet girl, except on Fridays when she pays tribute to Sog the Hyena Spirit.
b) **Blin Snimen** A pleasant fellow, except his nose constantly leaks fluids that look almost radioactive.
c) **Bodkin St. Grille** A nice boy, but don't get him started about his extensive collection of human eyebrows.
d) **Larth Nud** The sweet guy always wears a smile. Because of allergies, he brushes his teeth with vinegar/ sardine toothpaste . . . when he bothers to brush at all.

You've been chosen as Principal for a Day! You're not only popular, but now you're powerful. With your new-found authority, which of the following changes at school would you enact?

a) All drinking fountains now squirt soda pop.
b) Skateboarding in the halls is encouraged.
c) New class schedule:
  Introduction to Video Games
  Advanced Messing Around
  Recess
  Intermediate Rollerblading
  Lunch
  TV Theory
  Ideas in Kicking Back
  Snack Time
  Telephone Calling Made Easy
d) No dress code
e) Better stereos on school buses

Ms. Gristle is taking your class on a field trip to Dino World, the dinosaur theme park for timid dinosaurs.

Yikes! Run for cover! A dinosaur has broken out of its high-security holding pen. Which of these misfit lizards is least likely to dine on paying customers?

a) Cryanosaurus Rex—This dinosaur looks ferocious but is very sensitive and prone to crying fits.
b) Nervousatops—This shaky, nervous fellow just wants to be liked.
c) Spinelessor Raptor—This guy has no backbone and is afraid of his own shadow.
d) Scaredycat-asauras—He just wants a bowl of warm milk and a quiet place to curl up.
e) Brontochickenus—A huge, squawking, easily frightened dinosaur. His feelings are hurt because he thinks nobody likes him. He's probably right.

Chapter Three

Extra-Credit Pop Quiz

Which of these methods is the best way to cure a hiccup?

a) Tickle an enraged ferret.
b) Drink a glass of water while stitching up a wound.
c) Breathe slowly into a small paper bag containing a spoiled ham.
d) Square dance with a live salmon.

Contest: Typing for speed and accuracy. Who would win?

a) Hercules
b) Samson
c) The Incredible Hulk

The local newspaper has chosen you as Chimney Sweep of the Year! Now they need a photo for the front page. Choose your photo situation:

a) You—in a dentist chair having a tooth pulled.
b) You—being given a headlock by your Aunt Chloe.
c) You—dressed as Neptune with a live squid as a hat.
d) You—performing the "Nutcracker" onstage as done by Forrest Gump.

Fresh Tracks

Track and identify these dangerous and mysterious animals.

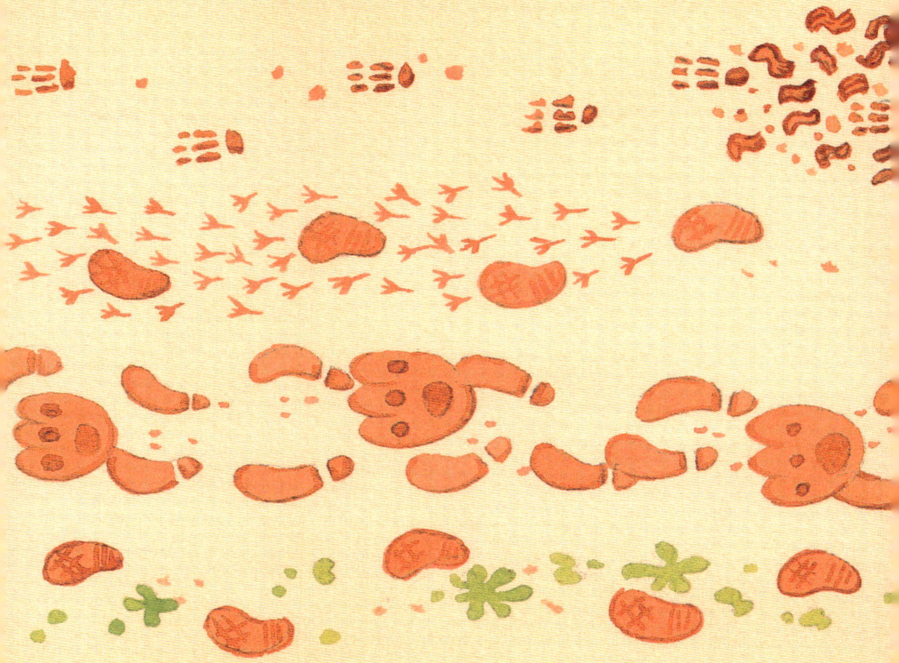

Answers
a) A kid with a leaky slurpy.
b) Barney the Dinosaur being chased by an angry mob.
c) A kid with all his eggs in one basket—and then they hatch.
d) A beaver on a wooden crutch who couldn't resist a snack.

Chapter Four

"I'm Telling" Survivor, the Home Game

HONEY

Dinner Rules!

The whole family is crowded around the dinner table, and the food looks and smells yummy! One problem: You're the Table Monitor tonight. That means that instead of chowing down like a starving beagle, you have to maintain order and discipline during this evening's feeding frenzy.

Read these rules to your family and let them know that you expect their complete cooperation.

First of all, starring contests and giggling are encouraged.

Rule #1 Any milk that shoots out of anyone's nose will be considered fair game and can be drank by any other family member.

Rule #2 All mashed potatoes are to be formed into a volcano and should be filled with lava (gravy or butter). As the lava seeps down the side of the volcano, the villagers (peas and carrots) shall be terrified and sacrificed to the Tiki God (you).

Rule #3 All spaghetti noodles should be tracked down as though they were venomous snakes and eaten individually.

Rule #4 When eating corn on the cob, you must make a typewriter bell "ding" at the end of each row.

Rule #5 Before eating black olives, they are to be stuck to the end of each finger and then wiggled at the person across from you.

Rule #6 And lastly, all food in your plate that you do not intend to eat should be chopped into microscopic bits and spread around your plate to give the impression that you gave it a good try.

Your mom is driving you and your friends to the mall. And she insists on shopping with you. Normally, that's OK, but this time she wants you with her so that you can try on clothes at the stores SHE chooses! Your friends are going to enjoy this. Choose three stores to patronize:

a) Turtleneck City
b) The Rayon Polyester Hut
c) Speedo Outlet World
d) Rhinestones-R-Us
e) Short 'N' Chubby Junction
f) Leisure Suit Barn
g) Ye Olde Pilgrim Shoppe, "clothing for pilgrims and their Quaker friends"

Smile!

Aunt Dorito, the health nut, has given you the jumbo variety pack of All Natural Toothpaste. "You'll love these! Try one!" she says. Help make Aunt Dorito happy by using one of these unique flavors of toothpaste . . . while she watches.

a) Extra Grainy Whole Wheat
b) Cabbage Mint
c) Guava Nut with Fluoride
d) Yam Gel
e) Broccoli-Carrot with Retsin

Rainy-Day Activity: Make and Bury a Time Capsule!

A time capsule is a fascinating way to show future generations how we really lived.

Here's how to do it: Find a box (metal is best) and fill it with everyday items that best reflect how we live today. Some things that you might want to include would be today's newspaper, a sandwich, a diary, a graded test, a video-game cartridge, a comicbook, pictures of you and your friends, and whatever else would best reflect our day-to-day lives.

Now bury it in a safe place. In the backyard. Under the dog house. Under the patio. Wherever.

The Next Day

After a brief ceremony, dig up the box and open it.

You'll marvel at the relics and trinkets that were clues to a more primitive lifestyle from a bygone age. You'll smile when you think about the simple, quaint life these people must have led. And you'll be nauseated if you try to eat the sandwich.

Dear Diary,

Writing in a Diary or Journal can be a good way to express your private thoughts about your crazy and complicated life. Writing can also be a fun way to sort out your feelings and keep your life in perspective. Your daily entries can be long, soul-searching narratives, or you can just jot down a few thoughts. Your entries don't even have to be daily. You can write in your diary every few days if that works better for you.

Your diary doesn't have to be just words. You can keep your favorite pictures, artwork, or ticket stubs in your diary, too. Have fun. Don't be afraid to be creative. But remember, your Diary is a personal journal, so keep it in a safe and secret place.

Just be yourself when writing in your Diary. Here are some sample Diary entries to show you how each person has his or her own style.

Dr. Frankenstein

October 29th

Dear Diary—Today I sent Igor out for another brain. And a pizza. He was late as usual. Fortunately, the brain looks like a fresh one. The pizza was cold.

November 3rd
Dear Diary—The villagers are angry again! But why???? What's a few missing brains and dug-up coffins to them? Pesky troublemakers!!!

November 4th
Dear Diary—My experiments are going well, but I need more power! My electric bill is sky-high and it's getting stormy outside. Lots of lightning strikes around the castle tonight. Hmmmm. That gives me an idea. Talk to you later.

Queen Elizabeth

Sunday, July 11
Yo! Diary,
Whew!! I am still soaking wet from the water-balloon fight with that nutty Duchess of Kent and that kooky Archduke of Wherever! And can they eat!! I thought I could shovel it in—but these two had sparks flying off of their forks! Gotta go!

Monday, July 12
Coming atcha, Diary,
I gotta get moving. I am off to another rodeo today, and then I'll be playing paintball later with President Bush. Where did I leave my skateboard? If I don't find it, heads will roll!! (I love saying that.) Later, gator!

General Custer

April
Dear Diary,
Ahhhhh! Another perfect day. My silky, golden hair is looking particularly heroic as the wind blows through it. I am easily the most handsome officer in this rag-tag army. Seems to be a lot of Indians around here today. As usual, they'll be no match for my troops and me. There's Geronimo. I wonder what kind of hair conditioner he uses . . .

Happy Birthday!

Your parents are determined to pass on their work ethic and green thumb. In other words, they want you to do all the yard work. As the designated lawn slave, pick one of these valuable birthday presents that your parents picked out especially for you:

a) Weed Tweezers

b) Lawnmower Wax

c) Racing stripes for your weedwacker

d) Personalized manure spreader

e) Glow-in-the-dark lawnmower dipstick

f) A carrying case for your new hedge clippers

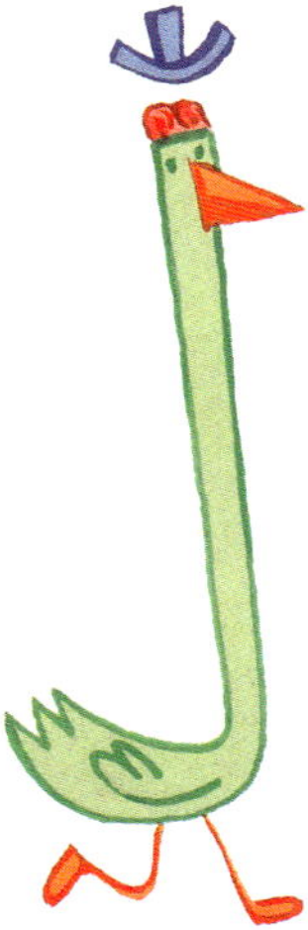

It's time for the annual Father-Son Picnic. You must enter at least one of the following contests of skill:

a) The Father-Son Three-Legged Race. They actually skin-graft your left leg and your father's right leg together, and then you have to sprint to the 7–Eleven and back.
b) The Porcupine Toss.
c) The tag-team Pie-Eating Contest. Choose your pie: Liver or liver and onions.
d) Bobbing for Thorns.
e) Dodge the Rotten Eggs.

The family that plays together stays together. But sometimes work has to get done. While typical chores and manual labor are usually beneath you, for the sake of family harmony, you've got to do something to show that you're willing to pitch in. No problem. You are always willing to make a sacrifice for the good of the family. Choose one of the se grueling chores:

a) You are gracious enough to test all the telephone lines (by calling your friends) and making sure they are in proper working condition.
b) You are willing to set aside some of your valuable time and check the *TV Guide* for accuracy.
c) You don't mind taking a little time out of your busy schedule to make sure that the cookies and potato chips are fresh and unbroken. You will dispose of broken or cracked chips and cookies in your own way.
d) You are willing to sleep longer so that family members can use bathrooms and showers in the morning without being interrupted.

Summer vacation means road trips. You'll be spending the next $4\frac{1}{2}$ hours hurdling down the Interstate in a cramped car. You and your family will be wedged in like sardines. Destination: Cape Grunion National Park.

You're the last one to get in the car, and you'll have to choose who you'll sit next to for the entire trip. By the way, your Walkman is broken.

a) **Grandma** She's got a chunk of banana the size of a half dollar stuck on her upper lip, and she loves talking about the "old days." She hates "new-fangled contraptions."
b) **Sister** "I'm telling!" is her favorite phrase. She insisted on bringing her favorite doll, Baby, Wets All The Time. And she will need help with all of the wet diapers.
c) **Brother** Perfected the art of the noogie, wedgie, and ear-flicking. Has the I.Q. and sensitivity of a warthog. He could use your advice about his skin problems, though.
d) **Your sister's strange friend, Tiffany** Smells like a bucket of peach perfume. She adores you and laughs nervously at everything you say. Even when you cough or sneeze. Stares at you a lot.

Wake Up!

The smoke alarm is sending a piercing, shrieking wail through the house and that can only mean one thing:

FIRE!

Your family and pets are all safe outside and are waiting for you. Quick, you have only seconds to grab *one* thing in your room and then get of the house. Pronto! Here are your choices:

a) Your favorite CD—"The Armenian Polka Dance Craze"
b) Your prized collection of mustache combs
c) Your favorite book, *The Magical World of Dry Skin*
d) Your unfinished science project: A working model of the human respiratory system made from sweaty headbands
e) Your live hornet's-nest-and-starfish windchime

It's Bring Your Child to Work Day and—Surprise!—your mother has chosen to bring you to spend the day with her and her interesting co-workers. Choose her place of employment:

a) The Associated Fork-Sharpening Warehouse
b) Clamatoes, a trendy clam, tomato-and-vinager beverage canning factory
c) Screen by the Yard Outlet Store
d) The Gravel Emporium
e) Mop and Broom Haven

Uh oh! Here comes Uncle Lars and his family. Lucky you, they'll be staying at your house for the next three days. They're nice enough people, but they didn't exactly sprout from the smartest branch of the family tree. During their stay, one of them will have to sleep on the floor in your room. Choose one:

a) **Gretel** Honking like a foghorn because of a nasal condition, Gretel sleeps in an oxygen tent and needs total and absolute quiet. Also, do you mind keeping her dehumidifier full of water during the night? Thanks.

b) **Dobie** He's a walking, talking collection of of corns warts, warts and strange bumps. And he has a story to share about each one.

c) **Uncle Lars** Breathes only through his mouth. But his crooked front teeth are spaced apart in such a way that he whistles every time he breathes. He insists on knowing how much everything costs, how you spend your allowance and why. Loves to talk, hates to listen.

d) **Aunt Budgey** Nervous and wiry. She not only loves birds—she looks like one. But she doesn't eat like one. Hide all the food, especially the sweets. She'll eat through the night and just loves crunchy snacks.

It's time for the Family Olympics! Show your family pride by going for the gold in at least two events:

a) **Haircut Relay** You and your near-sighted grandfather give each other lightning-quick haircuts using sheep-shearing clippers.
b) **Garbage Toss** Heave colossal bags of rotting garbage from your front door into the stained and dented garbage cans at the curb.
c) **High Hurdles** Dash and leap over small siblings and the family pets as you race other family members to the kitchen for the last brownie.
d) **Remote-a-Thon** You and the other "athletes" battle for television supremacy using cunning, guile, and super-quick thumbs.

Chapter Five

Celebrity Split Ends

Elvis Presley's records frequently went Platinum. Although he recorded some incredibly popular songs, he made a few duds, too.

None of these songs went platinum, gold, or silver. They went straight to the trash can. Can you put these Elvis tunes in order from bad to worse?

a) "Outhouse Rock"
b) "I Wanna Be Your Cold Sore"
c) "All I Need Is My Medication"
d) "Let Me Be Your Illiterate Pen Pal"
e) "Blue Suede Support Stockings"
f) "The Angriest Wedgie"
g) "The Hair Club for Men Blues"

It's all in the name.

Did you know that John Wayne's real name was Marion Michael before he changed it for Hollywood? The names people have can sometimes help define who they are. And sometimes NOT.

Match these famous folks in history to their real names:

a) Pablo Picasso
b) Ghengis Khan
c) Napoleon Bonaparte
d) Christopher Columbus
e) Babe Ruth
f) Chief Sitting Bull
g) Henry VIII

1) Drabby Topnot
2) Bagette Grubb
3) Chief Shivering Mole
4) Melvin III
5) Harwell Ratneck
6) Percival Khanstance
7) Slorthen Nooge

Celebrity Tattoos

Fads come and go, but tattoos are here to stay. Literally. Match each of these famous folks to his or her unlikely tattoos.

a) Mona Lisa

b) Pablo Picasso

c) Betsy Ross

d) Lewis and Clark

e) Barney the Dinosaur

f) Martha Stewart

g) Charles Darwin

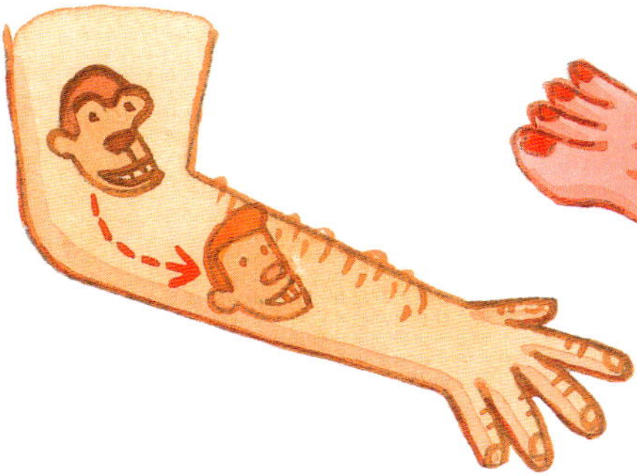

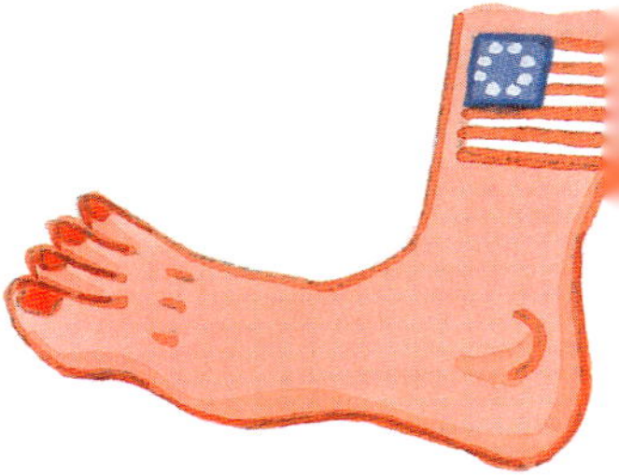

Mother
smile
BORN TO ANNOY

Who would win?

Full-Contact Spelling Bee:
Abe Lincoln vs. George Washington

Words from the Wise

For some people, the road to fame was paved with witty and wise sayings. Match these great orators to their quotable quotes.

a) Abe Lincoln
b) Cleopatra
c) Janet Reno
d) Margaret Thatcher
e) Richard Nixon
f) Mother Theresa
g) George Washington

1) "Act your age—not your shoe size!"
2) "If you love it so much, why don't you marry it?"
3) "Take a picture; it'll last longer"
4) "It's all fun until someone loses an eye!"
5) "That's so funny I forgot to laugh."
6) "I know you are, but what am I?"
7) "Mind your own beeswax."

You have been nominated to run for President of the United States!! Your parents are so proud. Now you'll be rubbing elbows with the rich and famous. But it's not enough to just have a great time at fundraisers and banquets. It's time to roll up your sleeves and get to work. What you need is a campaign slogan that will unify your message and captivate America's imagination.

Pick a winner:

a) "Read my lips: Pass the donuts!"
b) "I'll be in the presidential swimming pool if you need me."
c) "I'll be at my desk at the crack of noonish."
d) "Vote for me! Let's see what kind of mess I can get us into."
e) "I'll move the White House near a beach."

One way to tell if "you've arrived" is to have your life story told on the big screen or on TV. The Biography Channel has contacted you and plans to do a one-hour special based on your life. They've done hours of interviews with you, your friends and family and have all the information. Now they need a snappy title for the film. They want your opinion. Choose one that best sums up your life so far:

a) "Vegetables, Schmegetables! Who Needs 'Em! My Life as a Daredevil!"
b) "It Was Broken Before I Touched It! My Story of Courage"
c) "My Never-Ending Search for More Candy"
d) "How I Made Our Home a Zoo"
e) "Life in the Backseat of a Van"

You've saved an internationally celebrated group of entomologists from certain discomfort by directing them away from an aggressive swarm of monarch butterflies.

You're a hero and an instant celebrity! Not only do you get a key to the city, but they are renaming that species of butterfly in your honor. Choose a scientific name:

a) *Cranial maximus*
b) *Nosepickus toomuchus*
c) *Slumbera lateca*
d) *Ramma foodicus ina mouthial*
e) *Rarelyias studycus*

Chapter Six

Final Exam

You have lost your hand in a horrible whaling accident. The doctor must fit you with one of the following implements . . . choose one:

a) A fake foot
b) A flashlight that never turns off
c) A realistic hand clutching a baby bottle
d) A bionic hand that involuntarily raises and snaps its fingers as though hailing a waiter

Four out of five dentists agree: After Halloween, Easter is a time when most kids eat too much candy. Help yourself to a healthful holiday by choosing two of the taste sensations below.

a) A giant, hollow ricecake bunny
b) Alpha-alpha-filled candy eggs
c) Free-Range M&M's
d) Tofu-iced cupcakes
e) Spinach & Peanut Butter Eggs
f) Malted Skim-Milk Balls

You are marooned on a deserted tropical island in the South Pacific. Through some quirk of fate and very dependable mail delivery, you can receive up to two weekly periodicals.

Choose two:

a) *Igloo Illustrated*
b) *Taxidermy Weekly*
c) *The Snowshoe Chronicle*
d) *Snowplow Times*
e) *Iceberg Magazine*
f) *Litterbox Gazette*

As mad scientists go, you're one of the nuttiest. While other mad scientists seek world dominance, your plan is to conquer and control the minds of the townsfolk of Rugburn, South Dakota. But how you plan on starting your evil empire is the question.

Choose one of the four options below:

a) Send mind-control signals through Marsha Brady's braces.
b) Gigantic, Robotic Hedgehogs.
c) Send them thousands of gift packages of Candy Corn, wait for the sugar high to kick in, then they'll be putty in your hands.
d) Secretly remove the vowels from all their keyboards and typewriters. The result will be maddening frustration and eventually they will be disoriented and docile. Then you make your move.

It seems that each culture has its own unique superstitions. According to some people, if you break a mirror you may be looking forward to seven years of bad luck. Which of the superstitions below are still observed:

a) Walking under a burning bridge will bring bad luck.
b) If two sloths are seen riding a yak to church or synagogue, you can expect a rainy week ahead.
c) If you spill hot tar, throw some over your left shoulder for luck.
d) If a barn owl builds a nest in your trouser pockets, discontinue all plans to build an ark.

Wrapping Up

Silly questions are fun to ponder but they're also fun to create. Anyone can make up his or her own mind-boggling, important questions. You just have to be naturally curious.

For instance, everyone knows that an octopus has eight arms (tentacles). But can an octopus be left- or right-handed (tentacled)? Would they wear wristbands or ankle bracelets? If an octopus got cold, would he wear gloves or socks? The questions are almost limitless. You and your friends have an endless supply of material. Any person, place, thing, or situation can be "boggled" by these silly questions.

We're fortunate that many of life's important questions can be answered by opening a book or by surfing the web. But it's also nice to know that to answer some questions, you need to open your mind and imagination.

Index

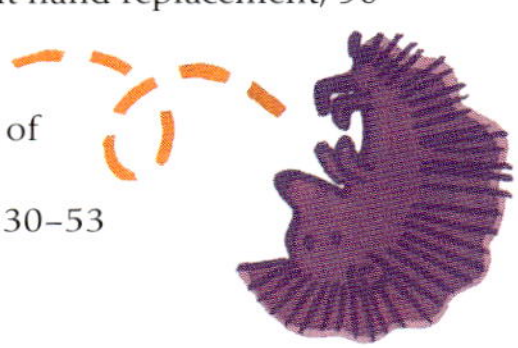